T0193155

Coming Back To Life

Valencia Hardaway

AuthorHouse™
1663 Liberty Drive
Bloomington, IN 47403
www.authorhouse.com
Phone: 833-262-8899

This book is printed on acid-free paper.

ISBN: 978-1-4567-5813-4 (sc)
ISBN: 978-1-4817-6787-3 (e)

Print information available on the last page.

Published by AuthorHouse 10/30/2021

author**HOUSE**®

[DEDICATION]

I would like to dedicate this book to my Heavenly Father for giving me another chance to live.

Contents

Introduction

I was about 12 or 13 when I asked God to show me a miracle. My exact words were, "God, bless me with a miracle, so that the world will see your goodness through me." I read about miracles, but never saw one nor experienced one for myself. Needless to say, I had no idea what I was asking for. God would show up, some ten years later, in a way that I could never have imagined. When I asked God for a miracle, I was sincere. Be careful what you ask for, because God's ways are not our ways, and His thoughts are not our thoughts.

Saving Power

I had a dream. I was in a cave-like dungeon. It was dark, but not too dark to see. Dirty water came past my knees. I couldn't see myself in the dream. I was on the outside looking in.

As I stood there, I saw fire and all shapes and forms of evil people and creatures. Something white as snow was gliding through the water like a snake. No matter how dirty and filthy the water was, the white object was never stained. It was a being more superior and larger than all the others present. He had the eyes of pure evil, disfigured in appearance, and was the scariest thing I have ever seen. It was no doubt that he was the one in charge. I realized I must be in hell. Suddenly, I could hear screaming, yelling, and all kinds of horrible sounds. The evil beings grabbed a white garment and took it over to the superior one. It became someone wearing a white hooded garment.

One of the evil beings snatched the hood off, and all I could see was a glorious crown. The crown was made of pure gold and sat so high on His head that I never saw the face of the person wearing the crown. Inside the crown were gems that made up the walls of heaven. The gems filled the crown, and I knew that the person wearing this crown was Jesus.

When I awoke, I fell to my knees and prayed. I was terribly frightened. It was one of those dreams that felt so real. I had no idea that this dream would be a revelation in my life. Jesus would come, many years later, and snatch me from the pits of hell and death.

Life More Abundantly

My father, Walter, used to call me the Bible carrier. When I wasn't reading the Bible, I carried it all over the house. I was so in tune with God's word, I could literally hear his voice speaking to me. Oh, how I took that for granted.

As a child, I was never sick, other than the common cold. Throughout high school, even though I was a cheerleader, I battled my weight. I was always trying to find a way to lose weight. I had family members, mostly adults, comment on how "healthy" I was. No matter how hard I tried, I could never seem to lose the weight. I prayed for weight loss, but not the way I would lose it years later.

I graduated from McNair Senior High School in Atlanta, Georgia, in 1988. I went to DeKalb Beauty College and finished within one year, earning my license in Cosmetology.

Immediately after receiving my license, I went to work at Xavier's Hair Design, in Decatur, Georgia. Everything was great. I worked with a lot of really good people.

One night, after leaving the salon, I had a dream. In my dream I was styling a customer's hair. My customer told me that Jesus was coming back, and when I saw him I would get only one chance to recite the prayer of repentance.

I asked her to recite it to me, so that I could write it down. I wanted to make sure I wouldn't forget. Automatically, I thought about the dream I had before and asked God, "What are you trying to tell me?"

Months passed, and I met a walk-in customer in the salon. Since I was the new kid on the block, I was chosen to work with her. After her shampoo, I began to style her hair. She was a God-fearing woman, and she spoke with so much conviction. She mentioned a prayer of repentance.

Instantly, my hands began to shake and I stepped back, with my mouth open. I could not speak for several seconds. I started thinking to myself, how did she know? I just met her. After I composed myself, I walked in front of her and told her about my dream. She told me that was confirmation from the Holy Spirit and began praying with me in the salon. I had no idea that God was preparing me for the most difficult and devastating time of my life.

My aunt also worked at Xavier's. After working there for a year or so, we decided to open our own salon in 1993.

It was called D&V's on Candler Road, in Decatur, Georgia. By then, I had started working part time at Georgia Institute of Technology. I was a Rambler at Georgia Tech. A Rambler was a person who worked temporarily or on assignment. I didn't need the extra income, but I liked the idea of having more money than I needed. It made me feel secure. Georgia Tech had departments all over campus that needed people to work for short-term and long-term assignments. Nothing could get any better than this.

My aunt and I started out with nothing, but we worked together and fixed our place up nicely. With the support of our family and friends, and a very busy, well known and easily accessible location, business was bound to be a success.

I moved out my mother's (Rosa) home and rented an apartment. I was 23 years old. My mother wasn't too happy, considering the fact that my oldest sister, Kim, had already moved out and I was next. It's four of us, and I was next to the oldest.

The hardest thing for my mother to accept was the location of my apartment. It wasn't around the corner.

I was part owner of my own business, doing something I absolutely loved, and had a part-time job on the side that provided me with playing money. On top of all that, I had a place of my own. I was on top of the world.

Deteriorating

I was never a person who made regular bowel movements. Some people are regular. They go in the mornings or at night. I went, but never every single day. But in August of 1993, I began going more frequently.

One day, while styling one of my clients' hair, I began feeling sick to my stomach. I politely excused myself and, once out of her sight, ran as fast as I could to the restroom. I didn't want my client to know I was sick. I didn't feel well, but I knew I could finish the job because I was a fast worker. I prayed and asked God to give me the strength to make it through the hairstyle. I got myself together and came out with a smile. I finished as quickly as I could and went home. I prepared dinner and before I could finish eating the last fork-full, I was running to the bathroom with diarrhea. When I wiped, I noticed blood on the tissue. My first thought was that I must need to drink more water. But no matter how much water I drank or what I ate, the blood would not lessen.

Even right after eating crackers, I ran to the restroom with diarrhea. Nothing would stay down. Blood was always present. Fear gripped my heart, and I knew I had to go to the doctor. The next day, I called my primary care physician and made an appointment. My mother thought it wasn't anything to worry about. It wasn't until much later that she realized the magnitude of my illness.

In November of 1993 I was referred to a colon and rectal doctor. After the colonoscopy, I was diagnosed with IBD (Inflammatory Bowel Disease). Inflammatory Bowel Disease is a group of inflammatory conditions of the small intestine and colon. The main types of IBD are Crohn's disease and ulcerative colitis.

I continued to work at the salon and Georgia Tech, even though it began to get increasingly difficult. One day I went to work at Georgia Tech and started to feel really bad. I told my supervisor that I needed to go to the restroom. With a smile on my face, I screamed on the inside. I felt so sick. I passed the restrooms on our floor and went downstairs to the restroom that had a couple sofas in it. I knew I had to lie down, but once I did, I couldn't get up. I reached in my purse, pulled out my phone, and called my mother, who also worked at Georgia Tech. I told her where I was, and she rushed over. When she found me, I was weak and lifeless on the sofa. I told her I couldn't make it back upstairs. She called my supervisor and let her know what was going on.

More frequently I had to excuse myself during hair styles. Sometimes, I would break out into sweats and have to lie on the floor until I could pull myself together to go back out and act like nothing was wrong. I didn't want my clients to know how sick I really was. Besides, I had a new car loan, rent and the salon to worry about. Now wasn't the time to get sick, but I didn't know how long I could keep this up.

The office visits to the doctor were very painful. I thought, Lord, why me? I was given medication, but the medication didn't work. So a week later, I went back to the doctor's office, enduring more painful exams. I was awake for every rectal exam. I begged the doctors to put me to sleep. I was back and forth to the doctor's office, changing medication every week, because the medication still did not work. I had several doctors out of the same office. As I made trips to the doctors' office, I was constantly passing blood from my rectum. I went from having blood in my stool to bloody diarrhea. I began sleeping a lot, not eating much, and running to the restroom, whether I ate anything or not.

Over the next several months, I passed an enormous amount of blood. The blood never ceased. Surprisingly, my blood was never checked. Sleeping was all I did, with the exception of making it to the restroom every 30 minutes, passing blood both day and night. I slept next to a portable heater. Sometimes I would not make it to my bed. I would collapse on the floor, only to rest for 30 more minutes before I could regain enough strength for the next episode. I was weak, nauseated, cold, and my lips began to turn pale. I stopped eating and started losing weight.

I had to give up my apartment because I was staying at my mother's home. I had been on my own for only a year and had to move back home, but I was too sick to care. By March, I couldn't work at either the salon or Georgia Tech. My aunt ended up losing our salon because she couldn't pay for everything on her own. I felt like I was losing everything I had worked so hard for.

My mother took me back to my primary care physician. Carrying me into the doctor's office, my mother thought I was anemic and needed iron medicine. When the nurse attempted to check my blood, she couldn't get a reading. She tried again and was unsuccessful. The nurse told the doctor that something was wrong with the machine, because she couldn't get a reading of my blood count. My doctor came in and took one look at me and realized the machine wasn't broken. I was totally dehydrated, and my blood count was dangerously low. My doctor told me and my mother that had I slept another day, I would have gone into a coma.

I was immediately admitted to DeKalb Medical Hospital, on North Decatur Road, in Decatur, Georgia, where I received 10 pints of blood. I was notified that I had ulcerative colitis, and my entire large intestine and a small portion of my small intestine were covered inside and out with ulcers. Ulcerative colitis is a disease that causes inflammation and sores, called ulcers, that line the rectum and colon. This disease affects men, women, and children and appears to run in families. Some of the symptoms are anemia, fatigue, bloody diarrhea, weight loss, rectal bleeding, loss of appetite, loss of body fluids and nutrients, and joint pain. In severe cases, people may have diarrhea 10 to 20 times a day. Crohn's disease causes inflammation of the digestive system and can affect any area of the digestive tract, from the mouth to the anus. Crohn's displays some of the same symptoms.

Surgery to remove my large intestine and part of my small intestine was my only option, but I would have to wear a temporary ostomy pouch. It took a week for the doctors to pump my body with antibiotics and medication, as well as the blood transfusions, to get me prepared for the surgery because I was so weak. "You will only have to wear a pouch for six to eight weeks, for healing purposes, then we can reverse it back to normal," the doctors said. "Okay," I said, but I didn't know what a pouch was. I had never seen one before, but I was willing to try anything to keep me from being so sick. And since it was for only six to eight weeks, I could deal with that. What is this that can destroy my entire large intestine in just five months? I would soon find out.

On March 16, 1994, my large intestine was removed, and I awoke to the worst pain I had ever felt in my life and to a pouch I knew nothing about. I felt as if I had been cut from one end to the next. "Oh God, help me please, pain," I said as I grabbed anyone in the recovery room who was within reaching distance. After the pain from the surgery became bearable, my whole outlook on my situation changed. I was disgusted and wanted the pouch off. I couldn't control what was coming out or when it would come out. I could not control the gas that blew my pouch up like a balloon. And the odor was retched.

My mother couldn't handle blood and anything gross, so I thought, I'm in big trouble. "Who's going to help me?"

A nurse came in with all these supplies. She wasn't just a nurse, she was an E.T. (Enterostomal Therapist) nurse. She had the softest voice and the magic touch. She changed my pouch, educating me and my mother. She made it look effortless. She was the first person to bring me deodorizer to put in my pouch, which made all the difference in the world, because it took away the odor that used to linger in my room for hours. Whenever my nurse was around, I knew everything would be alright. I hated to see her go, because I knew I would have to do it on my own and was afraid I would do something wrong.

My mother and I practiced and began to get the hang of it. I remember the first time we changed my pouch. Before we could put the protective powder around the stoma, I began to ooze. I panicked. Covering the ooze with everything we could get our hands on, I thought it would never stop. Then finally, it did. We cleaned me up and hurried to the next step of putting the paste on. The paste is what holds the appliance to my stomach. The appliance catches the waste. I was afraid every time we had to change my pouch.

I began to get so afraid that I didn't want to change it at all. As long as I was in the hospital, the nurse had to deal with it, not me. But I soon found out that the RNs weren't the same as the ETs. The ET nurses specialized in ostomy care. Most of the registered nurses I came in contact with didn't know how to change pouches, nor did they want to. They were quick to tell me, "I don't do that." And some of the technicians and nurses were so careless they left bowel contents on the outside of my pouch and just put the clip on, after emptying it, like it was okay. Sometimes they would get bowel contents on my gown and sheets and proceed to throw away their gloves and walk out. I had to stop one of the nurses and tell her angrily to get me another gown and set of sheets to change. It was around 4 a.m., and I had to get out of bed and clean myself, change and wait until she grudgingly changed my sheets. I was disgusted. I hated when that happened. I am very particular when it comes to my pouch. I like it clean and odorless at all times.

I told my mother what happened, and she began caring for me, even in the hospital. She knew no one else would do it. It was through her love for me and through prayer that God gave her the strength to change my pouch, but it was still hard. She emptied my pouch and urine. She measured everything and kept her own notes. She changed my sheet, gowns, and washed me up every morning. The nurses loved her, because they didn't have to do anything for me while she was there. I don't know what I would have done had my mother not been there for me during those horrible days. Every night, before my mother left the hospital, she would make sure everything was emptied. I knew that had to be very difficult for her. I later learned that she cried every day. This was my first operation. My nightmare had just begun.

Nightmare on North Decatur Road

It was indescribable. I began draining from my rectum. I began to get infections from all of the drainage I was having. I had to have numerous procedures because of it. Before the doctors could reverse me back to normal, infection set up on the left side of my abdomen. Operation number two was to clean out infection, only to have it return again and again and again. Every month I was having a major operation at DeKalb Medical Hospital.

My incision started from my sternum to pelvis. Each time I was taken back to surgery, I was reopened in the same incision. I was reopened so much that my surgeons had to insert bands inside my stomach so that my stomach would stay together. Before having time to heal, I was taken back to surgery. I was in the hospital when spring came, and for Easter, Memorial Day, Fourth of July, Labor Day, Halloween, and Thanksgiving. After a while, I thought I was never going to get better. I would inevitably wait for the chills to remind me that I was not going home today. I began to lose track of time.

Through that time, I had been admitted into the Cardiac Care Unit twice, because my heart rate would skyrocket. At the time my daddy worked in Baltimore, Maryland, for General Motors, so most of the time he wasn't there, but would talk with my mom and sisters about how I was doing. Well, in CCU I could feel him breathe on me. My dad was rubbing my hair and talking to me. He was in my face. I could hear him, feel him, but I couldn't respond. I couldn't tell him that I knew he was there. I couldn't open my eyes. He told me he loved me. I thought, Lord I must be dying, daddy is here. Walter never got in your face unless something was wrong. He lived in Maryland, and he was there because whatever was going on was bad.

My average weight was around 170 pounds. When I was admitted into the hospital, in March of 1994, I weighed 155 pounds. Within months, my weight plummeted from 155 pounds to a mere 98 pounds. I felt as though I was wasting away. With all of the constant bad news and all the surgeries, I began to get so depressed that my mother started emptying my pouch. I wished I was somebody else; anybody else other than me.

I had always wanted to lose weight, but never like that. My mother refused to let me have a pity party. When I came home from the hospital, Rosa made sure I put on clothes and sat up in a chair, downstairs in the family room. She made me get out of bed and walk. She didn't let me lie around. She tried to encourage me; all the while needing encouragement for herself.

When I came home from the hospital, I would stay in bed from the time my mother left for work until the moment she walked through the door, around 5:30 pm. I would lie there until I heard her hit that bottom step coming from the kitchen to the bedrooms. I would jump up as soon as she hit that top step and sit on the side of the bed, because I didn't want her to know that I had been in bed all day long. The doctors kept telling my mother that everything was okay. I didn't feel okay! She asked me if I had been up, and I lied and told her yes. That I was just sitting on the side of the bed. I didn't know if I was having a pity party or was I feeling really bad? The doctors said I was fine, but I wasn't feeling fine. I had been draining from my rectum for months, and had to wear a pad for the drainage, not for menstrual cycles. I didn't have a menstrual cycle for that entire year. I knew I was saved, and I asked God to take my life, because I believed I would go to heaven. I was tired of the hospital, exhausted by the surgeries, restless of the pain, worn out from all the tests, and I was disassociated from my ostomy; so much so that I wouldn't have anything to do with it.

My mother was trying to figure out how to care for an ill child, work, provide for her family, as well as be there for my other sisters. Melissa was the youngest and was a cheerleader in school. She had many games that my mother couldn't attend, because after work she would come straight to the hospital. "I would stay at the hospital until 11 p.m. or midnight, before I could leave her, and that was on one of her good days," Rosa later said.

Eventually, my mother quit her job at Georgia Tech to care for me around the clock. I felt horrible and like a burden on my family, but I couldn't do anything for myself. I took up so much of my mother's time that my youngest sister Melissa was neglected. Melissa was the only one of my sisters in high school. The hospital was Rosa's second home. She would camp out in the waiting room and push chairs together to make a bed. She washed her faced and brushed her teeth in bathrooms at the hospital, being there for hours and days alone. I wanted to die. The only thing I had to hold on to was God's word. Because I couldn't go to church, I had gospel tapes made. I would listen to the Mississippi Mass Choir and John P. Kee over and over in my tape player, which I kept on the side of my bed. That's the only thing that kept me from losing my sanity. Everyone has a song. Mine was "Your grace and mercy brought me through, I'm living this moment because of you."

I remember being in the hospital for Thanksgiving and coming home to see the Christmas lights and Christmas trees. Christmas has always been my favorite holiday, because everything is so beautiful and people seem nicer to one another. I thought I was home for good. I was home a little over a week, and then the first week in December, I was admitted into Saint Joseph's Hospital, on Ashford Dunwoody Road, in Atlanta, Georgia.

It was early on Saturday morning around 8 a.m. A friend of the family's had come up to sit with me while my mother and sisters prepared for another day at the hospital. I was glad to see him. I loved company and hated being in the hospital by myself. John was heaven-sent. He sat with me so my mother could rest, and that meant a lot to my mother.

My mother called when John walked in. She asked me if had I been walking, because I was breathing hard. I had not noticed any change in my breathing. Soon after speaking to my mother, my surgeon walked in and checked my breathing. Instantly, he told me I would have to move into another room so he could watch me closer, but when he mentioned ICU, I began to cry, because I knew ICU was a place for really sick people—even a place where people could die. I told John to call my mother.

As they were rushing to leave home, the nurses were rushing me to the ICU unit. Immediately after being placed in bed, I had doctors, nurses, anesthesiologists, and surgeons surrounding me. They were hooking me up to everything. I was given a consent form to sign in order for the doctors to perform emergency surgery. They began asking John questions. His mind went blank. I have never seen him so frightened. He couldn't answer anything. Every time they asked him a question, John would look at me, and I had to answer.

They were beginning to take me to the operating room when I yelled, "My family isn't here. Can I wait on my family?" "No!" they replied. "We can't wait." My mother and sisters weren't there, and I was terrified. As they were wheeling me down towards the operation room, my mother and sisters were running down the hall. I began to cry uncontrollably. They all kissed me, but the nurses had to keep moving. By the time I arrived in the operating room, I couldn't catch my breath. I began to panic and grab the nurses and tell them that I couldn't breathe. An oxygen mask was put over my face to help, but it felt like it was taking my breath away, and I kept trying to take it off. It seemed like forever before I finally went under.

I had a bowel obstruction, chronic pelvis sepsis, and a lower laceration along with other complications. I didn't know my heart rate was skyrocketing, a fever had spiked, and infection had spread to my lungs. That's why I was having a hard time breathing. This was the beginning of December of 1994, my seventh operation.

A Miracle on Ashford Dunwoody Road

I was placed on life support and had two more major operations. One was a tracheotomy. The Center for Disease Control became involved when my body would not respond to any of the antibiotics due to fluid in my lungs. I had a fever that ranged from 102 to 105 degrees for three and a half weeks straight. During that time I had to sleep on a cooling blanket. I had tubes and wires coming out of every place doctors could place them. I was tested for AIDS, because I was not responding to medication. When the results came back negative, doctors shrugged their shoulders. All the doctors, along with CDC, had done all they could do, and they told my mother to take me off life support. When my fever still had not broken and the doctors could not figure out what was wrong with me, the chaplain was sent to pray with my family.

It's so important for people to talk to their loved ones who are on life support or in a coma. I remember bits and pieces of my family being there, but I couldn't respond to them.

There was a time that I remember lying in the hospital bed, and my hands were strapped down. Nurses had my hands strapped down because I pulled a tube out of my nose. On this particular day, my mom and sisters came to visit me. They were all around me. I could hear them, but I could not open my eyes. My youngest sister, Melissa, asked, "Why are her hands strapped down like that?" I tried to move, but couldn't. I felt like I was paralyzed. I could just imagine what I looked like, lying there. My family was so sad. I could tell they were worn out with grief and exhaustion. No matter how hard I tried to open my eyes, they wouldn't budge. I thought, "Oh my God." I started screaming on the inside, "**I CAN HEAR YOU. DON'T GIVE UP ON ME. I KNOW YOU'RE HERE. KEEP FIGHTING FOR ME. DON'T LET ME DIE.**" I tried to jerk or move something, to let them know that I could hear them. Whatever I did scared Melissa to pieces. She got upset and began crying and asked the nurse what was wrong with me and why was I moving like that? Quite naturally the nurse gave me more medication to calm me down. **"NO!"** I shouted on the inside. "Please don't put me back to sleep," I said to myself. I didn't want to miss that time with my family. Most of the time, I didn't know they were there.

No matter how sick I was, my mom never stopped praying and could not take me off life support. Some of my doctors from CDC gave my mother the weekend to decide whether or not she would allow them to perform exploratory surgery on me. They wanted to open my chest and explore the inside of my lungs because of the fluid that was present. Her answer was **NO**. My mother truly believed that if she let them open my chest cavity to look into my lungs that I would surely die. She didn't believe that I could survive an operation of that magnitude. **"NO MORE SURGERY!"** My mother was adamant. "If you don't know what's wrong with her now, I'm not going to let you open her chest and play around with her lungs, like she's a guinea pig."

At that moment, my mother gave me back to God. All this time she was stressed out, exhausted, and holding on to me. Rosa told God, "Valencia was yours before she was mine and whatever your will is, let it be done." She knew there was nothing else she could do. There was nothing else anyone could do, even the doctors. My life, as it always has been, was in the hands of the Almighty God.

During this time, while in and out of consciousness, I kept having visions of a girl with long blonde hair. I didn't know who she was, but she was clearly visible.

When everything looked hopeless, God touched my body and after three and a half weeks of nonstop fevers, my fever broke. Halleluiah! By Jesus stripes I was healed. Afterwards, I learned that I spent Christmas and New Year's Eve in ICU, on life support, at St. Joseph's Hospital. The doctors informed my mother that they had to remove the trac before it damaged my vocal cords.

Once the trac was removed, they placed what looked like a cork of a wine bottle, in the opening of my throat. That was the beginning of helping me to breathe on my own.

During the day, I would have it removed to help me to start breathing on my own, but I was only able to keep it out for a short time, because I would have terrible coughing spells. When the coughing began, the technician was alerted. He would come in and stick this thin tube that looked like a straw down my throat to clean and clear it. The tube was used as suction. The procedure would always make me gag. I could not talk at the time and cried every episode. I felt like a piece of meat. I was treated like I wasn't human. I dreaded therapy.

I had some really awesome nurses, but you know there are always a few rotten apples in the bunch. A couple of nurses were not patient and were very insensitive, but for every bad one, God gave me three or four good ones. There was a nurse who shampooed my hair and put makeup on my face to make me feel better. Several nurses sympathized with me so much that if I were in too much pain, they would call the doctor, immediately, and give me more medicine. They couldn't bear to see me in pain.

I had a male technician too. I didn't like male techs, because due to having to a catheter, I couldn't wear underwear. The first time he came in shocked me, because the covers were pushed down and my gown was a little above my knees. When I saw him, I went to pull my gown down, but before I could do it, he began pulling it down for me. I jumped and looked at him with total surprise. It wasn't that he helped me pull my gown down that was shocking. It was how he pulled it down. He lifted my gown before pulling it down.

It reminded me of making my bed. You know how you lift the cover sheet that's on top of the fitted sheet, and then pull it down before tucking it under the mattress. That's how he pulled my gown down. Mind you, I had on no underwear, could not talk, and felt helpless. He asked me if I was alright and did I need anything. I watched him with a very puzzled look on my face. The second time he came in my room he pulled my gown down again in the exact same manner as before, but this time I was asleep. The breeze is what woke me. He startled me, and I sat up in the bed and motioned **NO** with my mouth. He knew I couldn't speak. **"DON'T TOUCH ME,"** I said firmly. He motioned that he didn't understand why I was so upset. I motioned for him to get out of my room and pointed frantically at the door.

The first time it happened, I didn't like it, but I wasn't sure if he did it by accident or on purpose. The second time, I knew he did it on purpose and would not get a third chance. During all the surgeries and hospitals I had been in, I had never experienced anything like that.

As soon as Rosa came to visit, I tried to write everything down about what just happened. She called the doctor and spoke with the head nurse, and I never saw that male technician again. Writing was the only way that I could communicate with my family, although they could barely understand what I was trying to say because my handwriting was so bad.

It was terrifying not being able to talk and tell my family when things weren't right. At times I felt helpless.

Not too long after that incident, God strengthened my lungs enough for me to come off the machine. The nurse placed a bandage over the hole that once held the trac. I asked the nurse for a telephone, because I wanted to be the one to tell my mother that I could finally speak. I called home and asked to speak to Rosa. My sister did not recognize me and gave the phone to my mom. My mother answered, and I asked if she knew who I was and she said no. I told her that it's me, Lynn. She started screaming and told me that she and my sisters were on the way.

Three and a half weeks later, I was released from the ICU unit onto another floor. It was now time to begin recuperating. I remember my doctor sitting in the dark, in the early hours of the morning, at my bedside. He told me that I was a miracle. Hospital staff came to my room to see the miracle everyone was talking about. I was one of the miracle children at Saint Joseph's Hospital. I felt so blessed to be alive and to be associated with the miraculous power of the Almighty God. I remember a cross over my hospital room door. Prayers went out, over the intercom, into the rooms of the hospital. I believe the Holy Spirit was and still is present in Saint Joseph's Hospital.

After being transferred from ICU, I could not walk, breathe sitting up, or get out of bed. I had to use a bed pan. At times, it was demeaning to have a nurse bathe me, like a child. But what could I do? If it wasn't my nurse, it was my mother bringing me a bowl to brush my teeth and bathe me, while I was lying in bed. The physical therapy was slow, painful, and grueling. I was instructed to sit up in a chair for only twenty minutes out of a day, and I couldn't do that. Every time I sat up, I couldn't breathe, and I would beg the nurses to let me lie down. I couldn't start walking until my lungs were strong enough to breathe sitting up. I remembered complaining about emptying my pouch, and now I couldn't even do that on my own. I looked towards heaven and thanked God for sparing my life and vowed that if He would let me live a productive life and be able to do simple things like go to the restroom, walk, talk, and empty my pouch, I would share my testimony with the world. Slowly I began walking and then pushing myself to walk more. I began walking once a day, then a couple times a day. I began pushing myself to the limit. Every time I walked, I would walk farther and longer than before. It could be 4 o'clock in the morning, and I would get out of bed and walk. I walked until I couldn't walk anymore. Once I crawled back in the bed, I hit the nurse's button and asked for pain medicine. After the pain subsided, I'd start walking again.

Due to long-term use of the catheter, I developed an infection which had to be lanced. To relieve some of the pain and help heal quickly, I had to sit on what looked like a bench inside a tub, with jet streams coming out of it. I had to fill the tub with the hottest water I could stand and turn on the jets. After a while, it felt like I was sitting in a Jacuzzi. Believe it or not, it really helped a great deal with the healing process. It became so relaxing that I began sitting in the tub at 2 and 3 o'clock in the morning. I found myself falling asleep sitting in the tub. The nurses began looking for me at all times of the night. I started telling them, "I'll be in the Jacuzzi if you need me." They would laugh. I had to find ways to cope with being in the hospital for so long.

One of my doctors told me that once I healed for a year, he would go back in and reverse the procedure and reconnect the stoma to the end of my small intestine.

Coming Back To Life

In January of 1995, I came out of the hospital with the will to live. My focus was on how to live with this until my reversal surgery. My first time changing my pouch, by myself, was at home, and a little scary. The opening of my first stoma was located at the bottom, and I couldn't see where to place the pouch, and sometimes it would leak. What if I couldn't put it on fast enough? What if I leaked? I didn't ask my mother for help. I knew this was a part of me, for the time being, and I had to figure out a way to live with it.

I was on the floor and had everything I needed to change my pouch. During the process, I called out for my mother. She came running and to her surprise, I was changing my own pouch. She was so proud of me and stunned at the same time. She couldn't believe I was doing it on my own. I wanted to show her that I could care for myself and that she would not have to change it for me anymore. Although I could now change my pouch on my own, my mother still wanted to help me. Without me asking, she would bring me warm, soapy water and an empty container, and she emptied my pouch for me. She would make sure the inside of the pouch was squeaky clean. I thought I was clean. My mother was cleaner than I was. She made me feel reassured. She always let me know that she was still there and everything would be okay. She was still willing to care for me, even though she knew I could handle it myself. That's a mother's love.

Spring was just a few months away. My sisters and friends of theirs were talking about spring break and where they were going. I remembered watching Spring Break on MTV the year before in the hospital. They looked like they were having so much fun. I said, "I want to go." My mother had a fit. I wasn't 100 pounds soaking wet and had just come home from being on life support. My mother thought if the wind blew, I would tumble right over. "No way are you going anywhere," she told me.

Everybody was buzzing about Daytona Beach. It was the place to be. I had already messed up Rosa's nerves, being so sick, in and out of the hospital nearly dying, so talking about Daytona Beach sent her over the edge. I told her that God had given me a second chance to live, and I wanted to live. I promised my mother that I would be careful, and my sister Stephanie told my mother that she would look after me. We went with two other girls who my mother knew. Even though Stephanie was three years younger than I was, my mother let me go. I was 24 years old with a new lease on life. Hey, make the best of it. The other girls knew about my ostomy, so I felt totally comfortable sharing a room with them. My mother rented us a car, paid for our hotel room and gave us money to eat with. We didn't have cell phones, at that time, so my mother prayed until we arrived in Florida and were able to call home and let her know we made it safely.

Daytona Beach was everything I thought it would be. The beach was breathtaking. All the college kids and bikers took over the strip. Melissa wanted to come, but had to work and stayed behind. Once Melissa found out how much fun we were having, she asked my oldest sister Kim to drive her down to Florida. At that time, Kim worked for Delta and never missed a day, nor was she ever late, and she couldn't take time off to drive to Florida and back. Kim thought about flying down with Melissa, but she didn't want to chance getting stuck in Florida. In spite of all this, Kim decided to make the trip. After work, she packed the car with Melissa's bags, and they started driving. They left home after 3 a.m. and arrived at the hotel around noon. Kim was tired, cranky, and pissed off by the time they arrived in Florida. She was irritable, because she was operating on no sleep and NoDoze medicine to keep her awake, had gotten stopped by the police for speeding, and had to turn around and drive back to Atlanta. She had to be at work by 7 p.m. that same day, and she wasn't about to be late. We begged Kim to stay in the room and get some sleep before getting back on the road. She nearly chewed our heads off and refused to lie down. My mother had the hotel room number and was frantically calling. We let her know that Kim and Melissa had arrived in Florida safely, and that Kim was doing a turnaround. My mother nearly worried herself sick until Kim returned home. Shockingly, Kim made it home in time to report to work, without being late. We couldn't believe it. That's when I realized how strong and determined Kim really was. Who could work all day and half a night, drive eight hours to Florida, and turn around and drive eight more hours, with no sleep, and then report to work for your normal shift? Needless to say, when she did go to sleep, she passed out for hours.

Daytona was one of the best trips of our lives. My sisters and I met a group of guys from Lagrange, Georgia, who occupied the room next door to us. I told them what happened to me, and how I had not too long ago been released from the hospital. No matter how much fun we were having, the guys would always check on me and make sure I was feeling alright. We had a blast.

Number 10

By the grace of God and with the help of physical therapy, I was able to walk again. And with the help of my ET nurse, and others, I was encouraged to live the life that God had given back to me. After healing for a little over a year, I went back for my 10th operation. My doctor was still optimistic and on June 3, 1996, I had my operation to reverse my illeostomy. After returning home from this last operation, I began to get sick again. I remember going to the restroom with the urge to push. As I began to push, something came out, but it burned. At first, I didn't know where it was coming from. I tore tissue and wiped front to back, and there was nothing on the tissue. I pushed again and brown substance came out, with a foul odor. Just like before, it would burn. I wiped again and nothing. So in the place that I felt the burning sensation, I got a mirror to see what was going on down there and saw a small hole, with brown substance oozing out. The infection literally burned a hole through my skin. I freaked. I called my mother and showed her what was happening. It was night time, so the next morning we left for the doctor's office.

When we arrived at the doctor's office, my main doctor was in surgery, and I had to speak with another doctor in his practice. This doctor did not have any bedside manners and didn't soften the blow. He told me the way it was and what he was going to do and what I would be faced with. He told me that I had a fistula and that I would be admitted into Saint Joseph's Hospital for surgery. He told me that I could end up with a permanent ostomy. It was too much at once. "Wait a minute, a permanent pouch!" I said. I had never been told anything about a permanent ostomy, but we knew I had to do it. "I'm getting sick again," I said, with tears in my eyes. My mother called my dad and others to let them know that I was being admitted back into the hospital. The doctor put the orders in place.

As soon as I was admitted, the gates of hell opened. The abscess burst and started flowing like the Mississippi River. "Oh my God, what's happening to me?" I screamed. The nurses started running and gathering sheets and towels to place under me. I went through so many that the nurses put me in the shower and turned the water on. They notified the doctor. We kept wondering where all this was coming from. I was still less than 100 pounds. My mother and I cried. I thought I was dying. While I was in the shower, the nurses, with the help of my mom, pulled off the sheets and changed the bed. As the doctors came in, the nurses took me out of the shower, cleaned me up, and put me back in the bed. As soon as my head hit the pillow, the nurse snatched the pillow from under my heard, put ice in my mouth and told me to swallow. The doctor proceeded to push a long tube inside my nose. He kept pushing and pushing until the tube reached down into my stomach. I didn't have time to object. It was painful and made me choke and gag. As soon as that tube hit my stomach, brown infection started flowing upward through the tube.

My stomach was pumped for three days. For three whole days, I had to watch the infection flow through a tube, from my nose, into a large container. I thought it would never end. It was nauseating. On July 29, 1996, only a little over seven weeks later, I had a fistulotomy, a surgical removal of an anal fistula, a tunnel-like lesion of the anus that causes pain, bleeding, and infection, which was my 11th operation. My surgeon came in and told me that it was time to choose between life and death. He told me that the poison and toxins in my bloodstream almost killed me before, and it was possible that I would have to live with this permanently. He wouldn't know until he got in there to see how bad it really was. My surgeon had my best interest at heart from the beginning, and I knew that he would do what was best for me, even if I had to live with a permanent ostomy. My surgeon never cut corners on my medical needs. He never suggested I see another doctor nor did he ever give up on me, so I knew he would do what was best. I said, "Okay." I trusted him. The only problem I had was that I never once considered living with a permanent ostomy for the rest of my life. My 12th and 13th operations took place on August 19, 1996, and August 21, 1996, for closure.

When I awoke after surgery, I had already been placed in a room. My mother was by my side, as always. I started feeling the side of my stomach, to see if the appliance was still there. As I kept feeling, I looked at my mother, and she started to cry. I stopped feeling and knew that it was permanent. We cried together. It felt like my first surgery. The only difference was that there was no turning back. This was never supposed to be permanent. There were no more surgeries of hope, thinking that some day this will all be over. I had been holding on to the day that I would have a reversal. That's what sustained me through all the surgeries.

It wasn't like it was new to me. I had been living with an ostomy for the past three years. I knew how to change my pouch and how to care for myself. The first thing I noticed, almost immediately, was the drainage from my rectum ceased.

I thank God for the prayers that flowed through the rooms and down the halls of Saint Joseph Hospital. I believed the prayers played an important role in my healing. Crosses were over the doors of the hospital rooms and a chaplain prayed for and with us whenever we wanted. They were just a phone call away.

My doctor sympathized with my family and had tried to reverse my pouch on several different occasions. I appreciate all he did for me, because now I don't have to live with thoughts of 'what if.' We tried everything humanly possible for me not to live with an ostomy. Reversals work for a lot of people, just not for me.

God doesn't make any mistakes, and I believe that God sent me a surgeon and other doctors who were compassionate and caring. God knew everything I would face, and I had to go through all those things to be able to accept my pouch today. I was so busy focusing on not living with a pouch that I didn't realize how much of a blessing it would be to me in disguise.

Dreams Do Come True

While I was in the hospital, recovering from the last operation, my vision of the girl with long blonde hair became a reality.

I was walking and while passing a room, I saw the same medication I had been receiving on a pole. I couldn't see the patient. It had to be God that prompted me to go in. When I walked in, I saw a young girl with long blonde hair. She looked to be in her early twenties. She was alone. I introduced myself as I shuffled in, pushing my own IV pole. She told me her name and that she was facing ostomy surgery, due to ulcerative colitis. She told me that she would rather die than live with a bag. As we kept talking, she told me the name of her doctor. I couldn't believe that we shared the same doctor. I told her that I was there for my final surgery, and that I had undergone ostomy surgery. I didn't let her know, right away, what I had just gone through. I didn't want to scare her. Plus, everybody's case is different. I assured her that everything would be fine. We shared room information and corresponding information. We talked about our families and if we were dating. I wasn't dating, but she was. She faced surgery within a day or so, and I assured her that I would be there with her, right before she went down.

She was so relieved to finally meet someone who understood her fears and concerns. The next time I went into her room, her family was there. They were warm and welcoming and excited to see she had someone to relate to.

As time got closer for her to go down for surgery, the more anxious and upset she got. She began crying uncontrollably. How well I understood. I had to be strong for her. I convinced her that everything would be fine and she wasn't going through this alone. Little did she know that I was dealing with accepting the fact that this was my reality and something I would have to live with for the rest of my life. I hadn't gotten used to that idea yet, but I had to be strong for someone else. It wasn't about me anymore.

I held her hand as she cried herself to sleep. When the nurses came to take her down, I stepped in the hallway and cried like a baby. "How can I be strong for her when I'm dealing with my own weaknesses?"

Right before they wheeled her out, I wiped my face and cleared my throat. As I walked in, I put on a smile. She was not afraid anymore. After surgery she had many questions. And after she was discharged, we remained friends. I promised to be there for her and was there for her wedding and the births of her two children. On her wedding day, her mother approached me and told me that she believed God sent me to help her daughter and she thanked me for saving her life. At that moment, I realized that she was the woman I saw in my visions while on life support. I truly believe God spared my life to help her.

Angel in Disguise

Before I was discharged, my sister Stephanie informed us that she was pregnant. I was ecstatic. This was our first baby. I had always babysat for others and gotten attached to their children. But this time would be different. This was our baby. I was in the hospital bed when I got the news. "I got him!" I exclaimed. I wanted to keep Stephon while Stephanie finished college and worked. I was so excited and wanted to get well so that I would be able to care for my nephew when he was born. It had been a long time since I had looked forward to anything. He inspired me to live.

Stephon was born on my daddy's birthday. I saw my sister give birth. I remember crying and examining him and counting his fingers and toes. "Stephanie, he has everything," I told her. I loved Stephon before he was born. I love children and always wanted children of my own. Stephon's birth made me focus on what was really important. I couldn't give up. There was someone who needed me.

As Stephon got older, I would periodically ask my surgeon about having children. At first, he told me not to worry about that and to get well. After a while, I asked him again and he said that due to all the surgeries and scaring tissue, that even if I could conceive, it wouldn't be a good idea. I was devastated. My mother wiped the tears from my eyes and told me that she would rather have me than for me to have a baby and die from complications. My mother was wiping my tears while fighting back her own. I never thought I wouldn't be able to bear children. I've always wanted to have children. After crying, I asked God to let His will be done and to help me accept and be content with His decision. I consulted another doctor about the matter and was scheduled to take a test at the hospital to see if my tubes were blocked.

That was one of the most painful tests I ever took. The doctor pushed the dye to the max, through both of my tubes. The pain was so severe, I couldn't even cry out. While the doctor was testing, I asked him if my tubes were blocked. He didn't want to answer right away, but I assured him that I was okay with whatever the results were. He told me that they were both obstructed. A part of me already knew the answer. When the doctor finished performing the test, I was instructed to get dressed by the nurse. She was surprised to see how well I handled the news. I told her that I prayed about it, and that God knew what was best for me. I had already gone through so much.

People believe that we serve a God who says yes to everything. Sometimes God says no.

The pain was so excruciating that when I stood up; I broke out in a sweat and had to instantly lie down. After I didn't come out, Stephanie came to the waiting area. I had to lie there for nearly an hour before I could walk to the car. God already had a plan. He knew I wouldn't be able to conceive, so he blessed me with the experience of motherhood through Stephon. I accepted the fact that I couldn't have children, but nothing prepared me for the dating game.

In the beginning dating with an ostomy had its challenges. I didn't know whether to tell him right away that I wore an ostomy or get to know him first. Some guys couldn't handle it. You know, the ones who can only see the physical part of you. The ones who want friendship with benefits. Before my surgeries, I'd always wanted to be in a committed relationship. I've always been the serious type. I didn't like to casually date.

After my ostomy surgery, I was terrified of dating. That's when my self esteem was low. I thought that no one would ever date me because of my ostomy. Would anyone ever understand? I built a wall around my heart. When I met a guy, I told him up front. I felt that it was better to get it over with, and if he didn't accept it, my feelings could not get hurt. I began to use my pouch as a weapon to keep men away, but I still wasn't happy.

I had always prayed for someone to love me for me. Well, he would really have to love me for me, literally.

I found that dating was the same for everyone, ostomates or not. If weight wasn't a concern, other issues were. Some men understood and some did not, but there was someone who loved me unconditionally, and my pouch was nothing out of the ordinary to him. His name is Stephon.

Stephon was about 2 or 3 years old when he began wanting to help me change my pouch. I had to hide my supplies, because Stephon would pour the protective powder all over him and stick pouches to his stomach. He said, "I want to be just like you, Auntie Lynn."

As I would empty my pouch, Stephon would always come in and want to help. He would help me change my pouch, as well. Sometimes he would use more than was required and squeeze out the paste and help me place the pouch on. He would also help me press the pouch down to make sure it had a good seal. Stephon was sent from heaven. I loved Stephon as if he was my own son. I was blessed with the honor of loving and caring for him while Stephanie finished school and went to work. He would wake me up in the middle of the night and ask me to make him pancakes. We loved breakfast food.

I heard about a man named Rolf Benirschke who played professional football with an ostomy. I had to meet him.

Just hearing about him inspired me. I wanted Stephon to see me as a strong person, a person with an ostomy who was meeting someone else with an ostomy who was living his life to the fullest and who gave me the encouragement I needed to keep fighting. Stephanie agreed to go with me to Rolf's book signing at Gwinnett Medical Center.

We sat in the first row where I met Raysa Abreu and her family. She was the 1999 Great Comeback Award winner, and another inspiration for me. When Rolf began to speak, I couldn't keep my eyes off him. Just looking at him, I couldn't tell he had ever been sick. As he told his story, he went on to talk about the Great Comeback Award. The Great Comebacks Program was established in 1984 to provide guidance and inspiration for people facing the physical and emotional challenges after stoma surgery (colostomy, ileostomy, and urostomy). Four recipients (one from the East, South, Central, and West regions) are recognized at special events across the country each fall, and the national winner is named. The recipients show other patients that they can lead productive and fulfilling lives with an ostomy. The award recipients receive a Steuben Crystal Eagle, on a stand with their name and the year they won the Great Comeback Award on it. The Eagle symbolizes freedom.

After he spoke, Rolf opened the floor for any questions. When he called on me, I began to tell my story. Everyone was amazed. I was encouraged to enter the Great Comeback Award contest. I left with a renewed spirit. I couldn't wait until I returned home to tell my mother all about the meeting. When I arrived home, I began writing my story. I mailed my entry the next day. I was told that the winner would be notified by January 2001. After January and February passed, I figured they had chosen their winner. I hoped I would win, but I had never won anything in my life, so why would this be different?

It was a beautiful day in April 2001 when I received a phone call. I looked at the number, and it was long distance. I answered and it was Rolf. The deadline had already passed, so I was wondering why he was calling. I asked him if he had chosen the winner, and he told me that he thought he was talking to her. My heart skipped a beat. I couldn't believe it. That was one of the happiest days of my life. That was the changing point in my life.

Rolf notified me of the different meetings I would attend and share my story. Each winner has a brochure made that tells their story. After I hung up, I remembered the day I met Rolf and how God always has a plan. All I had to do was walk in it.

The Winning Team

When I received the agenda for the first conference I was to attend, I asked if my mom could accompany me. The winner could take one guest.

My first appearance was in Portland, Oregon. We attended the Wound, Ostomy, and Continence Nurse WOCN 33rd Annual Conference from June 2–6, 2001. It was the ET Nurse's Conference. I was so nervous that I couldn't eat. Even though I had never spoken in front of a large crowd before, I felt honored to finally be able to thank the ET nurses for their dedication to caring for patients with ostomies.

On the way to the conference, I tried to tell myself that it wasn't a lot of people, maybe a couple hundred. When we arrived, there were around a couple thousand people. The Beach Boys were the entertainment for the night. I was taken backstage to meet the original members of the Beach Boys.

The Beach Boys entertained the guests at the WOCN conference.

When I was introduced and approached the stage all I could see was this bright light coming from the rear of the auditorium. Thank God for the light. It was so bright I couldn't see any faces in the audience. Not even my mother's. After I finished speaking, I began to walk off stage, but Rolf stopped me. I didn't know why. Rolf asked me if I could see, but due to the bright light on the back wall of the auditorium, where I had been focusing, I couldn't make out the crowd. As my eyes began to re-focus, I could see everyone in the entire auditorium was on their feet. I was receiving a standing ovation. There wasn't a dry eye in the house. Words can't express how I felt at that moment.

After I made it to my table, my mom hugged and kissed me. We partied the rest of the night with the Beach Boys. They were awesome.

Rosa and I were flown to our second meeting in Princeton, New Jersey, and our third meeting in Minneapolis, Minnesota, for the United Ostomy Association Conference. I was notified that the next trip was to San Diego,

California, on September 29, 2001, along with the rest of my family. I was elated that my mom, dad, Stephon, and sisters could all share one of the most memorable moments in my life.

September 11 is my birthday. I woke up feeling very sad. My heart was heavier than it has ever been. I told my mother that it was not going to be a good day. I couldn't shake the sadness. My mother thought I was depressed because I was getting older, but that wasn't it. I have never felt that way before that day, neither have I felt that way since September 11, 2001, but I would later understand why.

After the terrorists attacked, I wondered if they would cancel the 3rd Annual Benefit Gala in California, where I would be honored as the 2001 Great Comeback Award Winner. Security was heightened at the airport. I was never afraid to fly, but I was that time. But then I thought, security is so high that now is the safest time to fly, and my family and I are all together.

When we boarded the aircraft, the plane was nearly empty. Once the plane took off and the seat belt signs were off, my sisters and I went to other rows, where seats were empty. We all had an entire row to ourselves. My fear subsided, and we had a very smooth flight.

During our stay in California, I made appearances on television and on the radio station, and Rolf presented me and my family with tickets to the San Diego Zoo. Stephon really enjoyed the zoo, and we went swimming afterward.

We enjoyed the swimming pool at the Marriott.

I loved attending all the conferences, because they all had different themes. One of the conferences had a cruise theme. It was set up like we were actually on a cruise ship. The theme in San Diego was A Night in the Nile. There were belly dancers, and it was magical. I was presented with a Crystal Eagle with my name engraved on the stand.

During the summer of 2002, Stephon and I were featured on the Cutting Edge Medical Report, Living with Crohn's Disease, on the Health Channel.

On September, 24, 2004, I was asked to participate in a television advertisement and promotional video to celebrate the Great Comebacks 20th Anniversary. And on November 19, 2004, Melissa accompanied me to New York City, where we saw the video for the first time. My mother could not fly due to a cortisone shot that she received in her back. My mother had been with me all the other times before, and it felt strange not to have her there.

The view from our room in the Marriott Marquis.

My sister Melissa, Raysa Abreu, Rolf Benirschke, me, and Mary Benirschke.

My sister Melissa, right, came with me to New York.

Raysa Abreu, Valencia Hardaway, and Michael Nash,
another Great Comebacks Award winner.

Melissa and I stayed at the Marriott Marquis, in the middle of Times Square in New York City. When we watched the video, I couldn't hold back the tears when I saw the scene with my mother speaking. I missed her all the more. I was so grateful for Melissa being there with me. I couldn't imagine not being able to share that experience with someone I loved.

On February 27, 2007, my mother and I traveled to Washington, D.C., with our Great Comeback family. While in Washington, I brought greetings from the Greater Traveler's Rest Baptist Church to our former President, George W. Bush. I, along with other Comeback winners, also went to Capitol Hill, on February 28, 2007, to encourage the House of Representatives and Senate to pass legislative bill H.R. 1113, the "Inflammatory Bowel Disease Research Act."

Inside the White House with Great Comebacks Award winner Raysa Abreu.

President Bush posed with me for a picture.

President Bush and I inside the White House.

Inside the White House with President Bush.

The Great Comebacks winners and President Bush at the White House.

Congressman Nathan Deal posed with me. He is now the governor of Georgia.

Specifically, H.R. 1113 would focus on pediatric related research, genetic and environment based research into the cause and progression of IBD; clinical research, including translational studies and treatment trials; and support for the training of new investigators specializing in IBD. H.R. 1113 would also require the CDC to develop a "National Inflammatory Bowel Disease Action Plan." This plan would detail a comprehensive strategy for addressing the burden of IBD in both pediatric and adult populations and would create mechanisms for increasing awareness of IBD and preventing its progression and related complications, such as colorectal cancer.

Crohn's disease and ulcerative colitis, collectively known as inflammatory bowel disease, are chronic disorders of the gastrointestinal tract which afflict approximately 1.4 million Americans, 30% of whom are diagnosed in their childhood years. IBD causes severe abdominal pain, fever and intestinal bleeding. Complications related to the disease include arthritis, osteoporosis, anemia, liver disease, and colorectal cancer. We do not know its cause, and there is no cure.

I met former White House Advisor and Press Secretary Tony Snow at the Great Comebacks Award Dinner.

The day I arrived in the Capitol, February 28, 2007, I attended the Great Comebacks National Award Dinner held at the National Museum of Women in the Arts. I was honored to meet the former White House Advisor and Press Secretary, Tony Snow. Tony Snow was the 2006 Honorary Great Comebacks Award Recipient. Bob Schieffer, CBS News Chief Washington Correspondent, was the 2006 National Award Dinner Emcee.

I was also invited to Nashville, Tennessee, as a presenting speaker at the Crohn's and Colitis Foundation's patient education program on August 18, 2007.

I had no idea that my ostomy would bring so many blessings.

The Mob Squad

Although I could not have children of my own, God blessed me with my niece, Kayla, and my two nephews, Stephon and Stephen. Even though I was the only person in my family with an ostomy, Stephon, Kayla, and Stephen didn't seem to notice. It was normal to them. Kayla put on one of my pouches and told me the same thing Stephon told me as a child, "I want to be just like you, Auntie Lynn." It was very important for me to teach them and help them to understand who I was as their auntie and as a person living with an ostomy. They never looked at me as different or strange, nor made fun of me when I had gas. I knew, as they grew older, they would meet someone else with an ostomy, and I wanted Stephon, Kayla, and Stephen to treat others with ostomies with the upmost respect. It wouldn't be abnormal for them to have a friend with a pouch. They would be able to relate because their auntie has one and they know all about ostomy care.

Kayla tells me when it's time to change my pouch and believe it or not, she is always right.

All three of them would come in while I'm emptying my pouch if I didn't lock the door. They would walk right in and stand around me and the toilet like a group of physician assistants. Kayla and Stephen would argue over who would poor the deodorizer in my pouch and who would put the clip on. Afterwards, we'd all wash our hands together.

To this day, I have to lock the restroom door when I go in.

Celebrating Life Each and Every Day

On March 3, 2010, I was invited to attend the 25th Anniversary Celebration of the Great Comebacks and National Award Dinner at the Andrew W. Mellon Auditorium, in Washington D.C. My mother and youngest sister, Melissa, accompanied me.

It was a very special occasion, which reunited 20 of their alumni award recipients, along with professionals, lawmakers, and advocates from the ostomy community. I was delighted to see Rolf, the founder of Great Comebacks, David Johnson, CEO of Convatec, the world's leading ostomy manufacturer and a leading wound care company that partners with The Great Comeback Award, Suzanne Rosenthal, co-founder of Crohn's & Colitis Foundation of America (CCFA), as well as past and current winners. Suzanne Rosenthal was the original inspiration for the founding of the CCFA and is the co-founder and chairperson. Suzanne, along with Irwin M. Rosenthal, William D. and Shelby Modell, and Henry D. Janowitz, M.D., founded the CCFA in 1967.

Mary Benirschke, Rolf Benirschke, and me.

Mrs. Johnson, me, and David Johnson, CEO of Convatec.

Latoya Lucas, right, has been an inspiration.

I also had the distinct pleasure of meeting Latoya Lucas, an Army veteran and author who is a Purple Heart recipient and recipient of the Tony Snow Public Service Award. Latoya retired from the Army due to injuries sustained in Iraq. Latoya is an inspiration to me and countless others.

When I returned home, I collaborated with the CCFA of Georgia and my church, the Greater Traveler's Rest Baptist Church, in Decatur, Georgia, to form the first Crohn's and Colitis Support Group ever held in a church in Georgia.

My goal is to educate and offer support to anyone living with IBD, along with their family, friends, coworkers, as well as the community. I want to give others hope, confidence, reassurance, and show them that they can still live a fulfilling life with an ostomy.

Every day is a new day. I don't know what God is up to. My life has not turned out the way I planned. I have been on an emotional, spiritual, and physically challenging ride. Each day I am excited to see what God is going to do and what's in store for me. It was all in God's plan, and my life was and still is in His hands.

I am so glad that God doesn't give me everything I ask for. Had He taken my life when I asked, I would not have known that my miracle and healing was just two more chapters away. My deliverance was right around the corner.

My mother told me that about six months before I became ill, she asked God to increase her faith. She wanted to know, without a doubt, that God would perform a miracle, because at times she was doubtful, because of the unseen. Well, after thirteen surgeries and life support, my mother and I have seen God's miraculous power. God heard and answered both our prayers.

It has been over fifteen years since I was on life support. By Jesus stripes I am healed. I am thankful to be alive and for all the many blessings God has given me.

My mother says that if she had to do it all over again, she would. God was with my mother, through each of the thirteen surgeries and life support, building her faith and making her stronger, each day. "I say thank you, Father, for giving me back my daughter and for giving her another chance at life," Rosa exclaims.

My prayer is that you are blessed by *Coming Back to Life* and find hope in your situation.

ACKNOWLEDGEMENTS

I would like to acknowledge God for His miraculous power and for specializing in things that seem impossible. I would like to thank Rosa, for giving me life twice (the first time she gave birth to me and the second time when she refused to let the doctors take me off life support), my daddy Walter, sisters Kim, Stephanie and Melissa, and John for being there every step of the way. I would like to thank my Aunt Mary who rubbed my aching back with baby powder as I lay in those hospital beds, along with the rest of my family. My grandmother for answering all my calls, at 3 and 4 a.m., when I couldn't sleep. Words can't express the gratitude and love I feel for my doctor and surgeon, Guy Orangio. He never cut corners, and always gave me his very best. He fought for me, alongside my mother. Prebble Smith, my angel and ET nurse, was that light at the end of a very long and dark tunnel. I know God has place in his kingdom for you.

Thank you, Rolf, for adopting me into your Great Comeback family and for the experiences that have changed my life forever. I would like to express sincere gratitude to all ET nurses and Crohn's and colitis foundations all over the world for their hard work and dedication. Sincere gratitude to Rev. Booker T. Moore, Rev. James Jones, and Rev. Jerry D. Black for your prayers, long hours spent at the hospitals, and support through the darkest days of my life. For everyone who took the time to pray for me, I thank you. I love you Vickie Key and you will never be forgotten.

Last but not least, I would like to thank Mary Ball and the CCFA chapter in Georgia for seeing my vision and for taking a chance, with me, to reach out to my community by uniting with my church, the Greater Traveler's Rest Baptist Church, under the awesome leadership of Pastor E. Dewey Smith, Jr.

Printed in the United States
by Baker & Taylor Publisher Services